NAVIGATE YOUR STARS

Jesmyn Ward

Illustrations by Gina Triplett

SCRIBNER

New York London Toronto Sydney New Delhi

Scribner
An Imprint of Simon & Schuster, Inc.
1230 Avenue of the Americas
New York, NY 10020

First Scribner hardcover edition April 2020

SCRIBNER and design are registered trademarks of The Gale Group, Inc.,
used under license by Simon & Schuster, Inc., the publisher of this work.

For information about special discounts for bulk purchases,
please contact Simon & Schuster Special Sales at 1-866-506-1949
or business@simonandschuster.com.

The Simon & Schuster Speakers Bureau can bring authors to
your live event. For more information or to book an event,
contact the Simon & Schuster Speakers Bureau at 1-866-248-3049
or visit our website at www.simonspeakers.com.

Manufactured in the United States of America

1   3   5   7   9   10   8   6   4   2

Library of Congress Cataloging-in-Publication Data has been applied for.

ISBN 978-1-9821-3132-6
ISBN 978-1-9821-3134-0 (ebook)

For my maternal grandmother, Dorothy,
the first storyteller of my life.
Born wrapped in a caul, given to prophetic dreams,
she sees beyond us, but never closes her eyes
to us. She holds her family near to her, always;
she navigated the darkest ocean and the
wildest mountain to do so. I love her always,
in this world and into the next.

NAVIGATE
YOUR STARS

Good morning, y'all. I want to tell you a story.

I grew up in a poor, rural, mostly black community in Mississippi. Both sides of my family, my mother's and my father's, have lived there for generations. When my grandmother was a child, she studied at a one-room school that her father built to provide education for black children. By the time she was in junior high, she walked two miles to a school next to the local Catholic church, where she studied math and reading and writing. When she wasn't in school, she worked in her father's fields, weeding and picking.

My grandmother's schooling ceased when she was thirteen. There was no curriculum for high school education, no teacher for the older children, in the 1940s. After she left school, my grandmother worked many jobs to support herself and, eventually, her children, too.

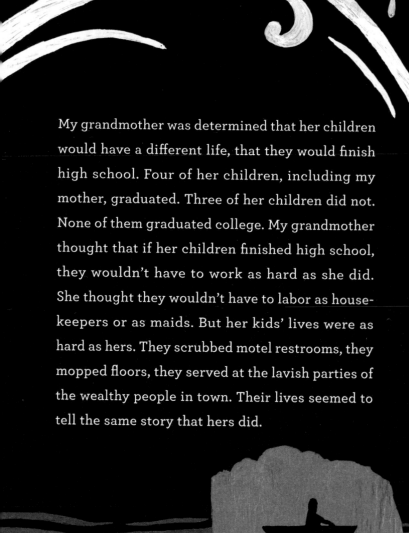

My grandmother was determined that her children would have a different life, that they would finish high school. Four of her children, including my mother, graduated. Three of her children did not. None of them graduated college. My grandmother thought that if her children finished high school, they wouldn't have to work as hard as she did. She thought they wouldn't have to labor as housekeepers or as maids. But her kids' lives were as hard as hers. They scrubbed motel restrooms, they mopped floors, they served at the lavish parties of the wealthy people in town. Their lives seemed to tell the same story that hers did.

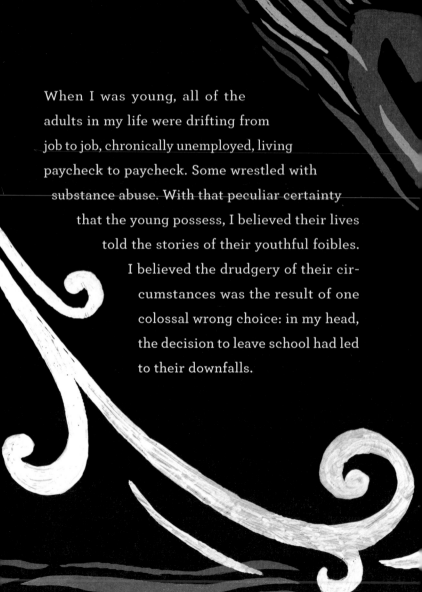

When I was young, all of the
adults in my life were drifting from
job to job, chronically unemployed, living
paycheck to paycheck. Some wrestled with
substance abuse. With that peculiar certainty
that the young possess, I believed their lives
told the stories of their youthful foibles.
I believed the drudgery of their circumstances was the result of one
colossal wrong choice: in my head,
the decision to leave school had led
to their downfalls.

I was determined to make better decisions. I would not live the rest of my life in my small, rural town, scrabbling for resources or working myself to the grave. One of the most important life lessons I thought I'd learned at the end of my high school career was this: the choices you make as an adolescent will determine your entire life.

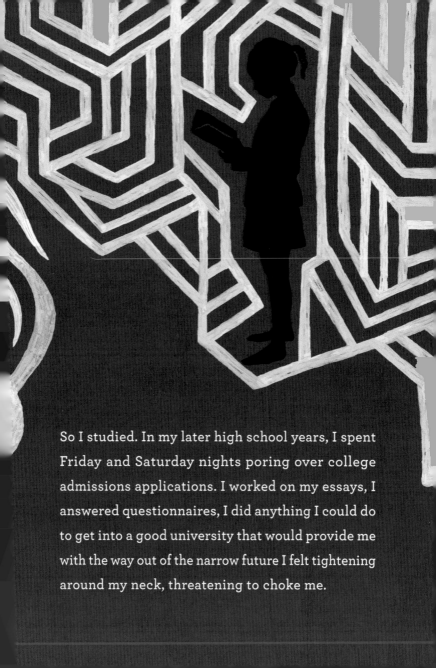

So I studied. In my later high school years, I spent Friday and Saturday nights poring over college admissions applications. I worked on my essays, I answered questionnaires, I did anything I could do to get into a good university that would provide me with the way out of the narrow future I felt tightening around my neck, threatening to choke me.

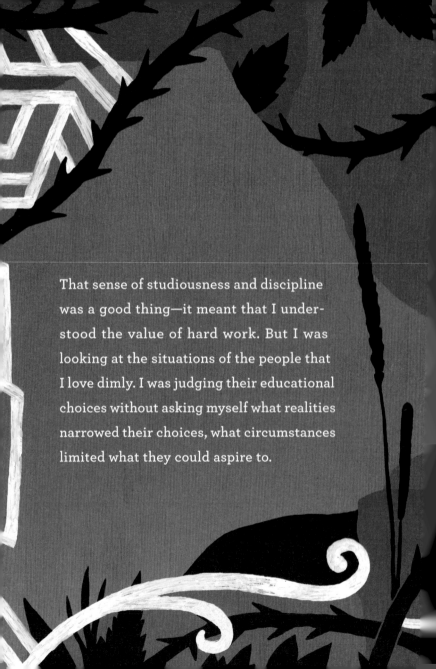

That sense of studiousness and discipline was a good thing—it meant that I understood the value of hard work. But I was looking at the situations of the people that I love dimly. I was judging their educational choices without asking myself what realities narrowed their choices, what circumstances limited what they could aspire to.

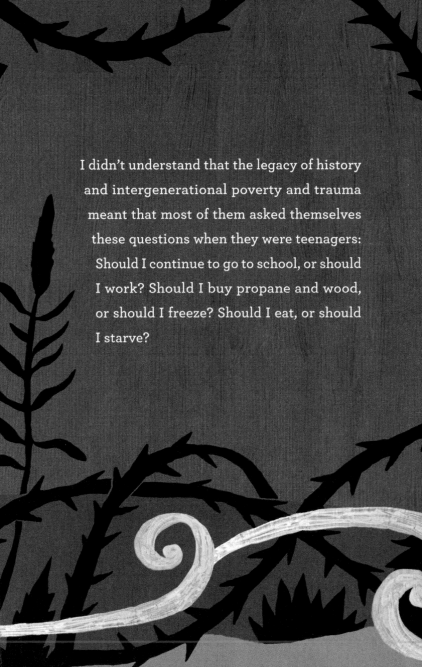

I didn't understand that the legacy of history and intergenerational poverty and trauma meant that most of them asked themselves these questions when they were teenagers: Should I continue to go to school, or should I work? Should I buy propane and wood, or should I freeze? Should I eat, or should I starve?

I didn't understand that writing a different story for myself meant that I had to not only make wise choices—plural—but have the gift of luck and better circumstances as well.

I didn't understand that my mother and father had given me an outrageous gift.

Unlike my parents and grandparents, I didn't have to choose between eating and my education. I didn't understand any of this when I matriculated to Stanford. All I saw was the promise of my one perfect choice: the promise inherent in education.

I was the child of cleaning women, bootleggers, factory workers, and landscapers. Of course the people in my family taught me the value of school. Of course they believed in learning as strongly as I did, given that education seemed like a magical key that would open the door to a life not bound by poverty, not restricted by the circumstances of birth.

My mother held the truth of this tenet close to her when she scrubbed floors. My grandmother held it fast while she stood on an assembly line for ten-hour shifts, doing quality control on endless processions of Pepto-Bismol and Maalox, and they told it to me nearly every day of my entire life. Before meals, before bedtime, repeated it like a prayer.

"You will go to college."

The subtext was this: You will be free of this drudgery, this tragedy, this mill. You will be free. And I believed them. I believed that one task, going to university, would be the key to changing the narrative, to escaping the legacy of being poor and black and Southern.

In college, I wasn't the standout student I had been in high school; instead, I was decent, even though I worked as diligently as I had before. University was much harder than high school; not only was the work harder, but the sense that I'd had in high school that I could study my way to a better life seemed confused. The relationship between studious effort and success blurred.

Instead of premed, or law, or business—something practical—I was drawn to literature and creative writing. I tried to study other subjects, anxious to see if I would feel the persistent burr of curiosity, the rush of passion, the reverence that came when I read poetry and fiction. I didn't. What would I do with this love for words that would not leave me?

Graduation came and went, and I had no idea.

I applied for job after job, and I almost began crying in a Macy's when the clerk ringing up my purchase told me that he too had been an English major in school. I thought I might try to be a writer one day, but in my early twenties I was no young phenom. I didn't even understand what a plot was. I attempted to write short stories but found myself with pages of extended scenes instead. My characters were flat and unbelievable; my dialogue was painfully fake.

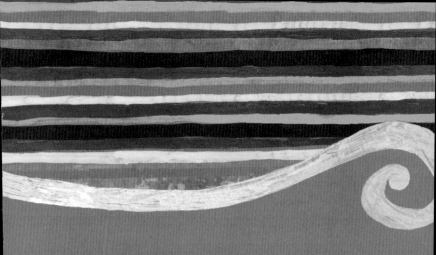

While my ambitious, savvy, assertive friends who'd majored in economics and political science were being snatched up for jobs, I was applying for positions in marketing and television and journalism and never hearing anything back. So after my graduation, I did the only thing I could do, considering I had no job offer, and no prospects, and only a passion for something I wasn't very good at. I moved home.

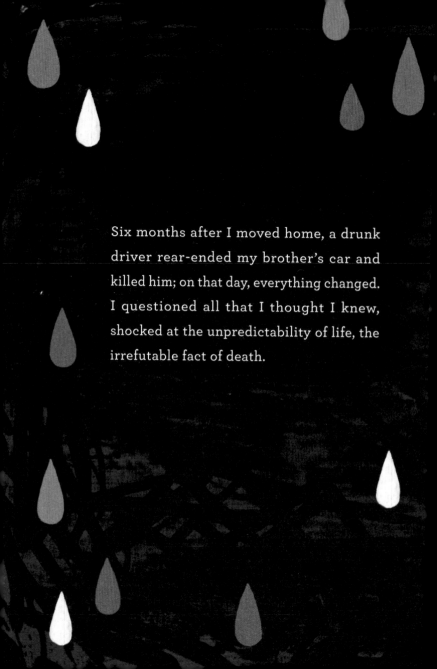

Six months after I moved home, a drunk driver rear-ended my brother's car and killed him; on that day, everything changed. I questioned all that I thought I knew, shocked at the unpredictability of life, the irrefutable fact of death.

I realized that a magic job wasn't going to fall into my lap, that my education was not the only choice to guarantee success, that sometimes life was hard without reason. So I adapted to my changed circumstances, just as generations of my family members had done before me. I did what I had to do: I applied for holiday work at a clothing store in a local outlet mall.

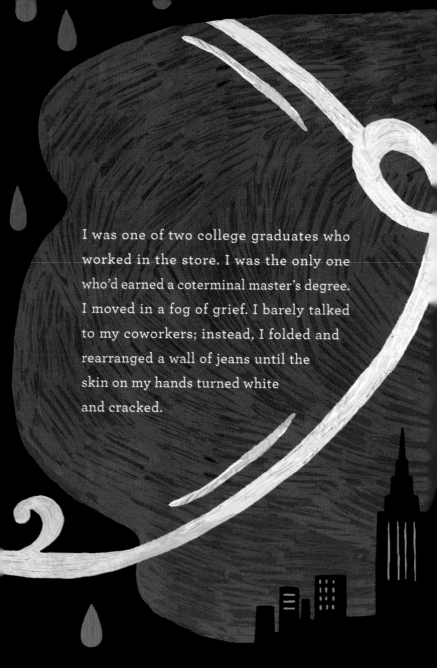

I was one of two college graduates who worked in the store. I was the only one who'd earned a coterminal master's degree. I moved in a fog of grief. I barely talked to my coworkers; instead, I folded and rearranged a wall of jeans until the skin on my hands turned white and cracked.

I spoke with friends who
lived in New York City,
and they encouraged me to
move there to search for work.
I was desperate, so I went and
interviewed for a job in publishing.
I worked there for two years. Surprise: I
wasn't a very good publishing assistant. I was too
depressed at my brother's leaving and too distracted
by that persistent need to write, even if badly.

At this point, I had a realization: completing university was not an ending, but instead was the beginning of finding my way to doing something meaningful. I learned that for most of us, there are no easy, singular ascents, and I realized I wanted to be a writer. So, I began to do the work. I made an important choice: I took a step. I read widely. I read contemporary writers who were unknown to me, and I read classic writers I hadn't read in school. I did as my grandmother and the people I love in my life did to survive: I adapted.

I made another choice, I took another step. I wrote bad poems that I hid from others, but I didn't attempt to write any more short stories. I realized I had only a dim idea of the conversation unspooling through the centuries that I was attempting to join by writing literature. So I read more, for two and a half years, I read, and at the end of that time, I wrote and revised one short story.

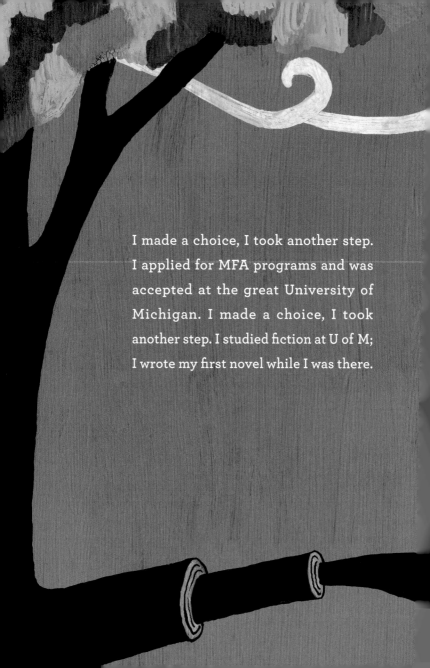

I made a choice, I took another step. I applied for MFA programs and was accepted at the great University of Michigan. I made a choice, I took another step. I studied fiction at U of M; I wrote my first novel while I was there.

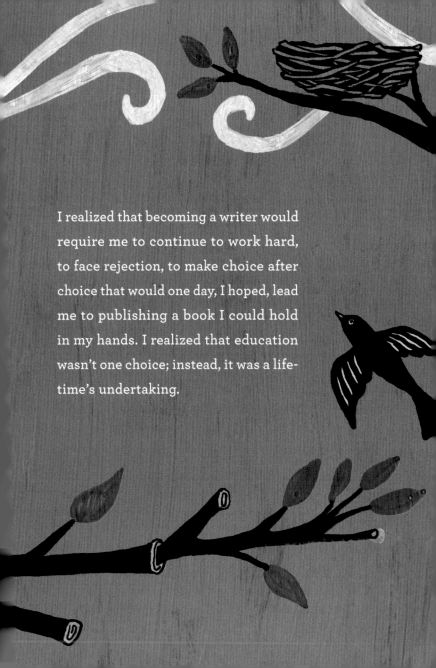

I realized that becoming a writer would require me to continue to work hard, to face rejection, to make choice after choice that would one day, I hoped, lead me to publishing a book I could hold in my hands. I realized that education wasn't one choice; instead, it was a lifetime's undertaking.

As an adult, I understand that finding the kind of life I want to live requires constant work, constant study, constant risk-taking, and that there are no easy paths to success for people like me. So for a decade, I made the best choices I could. I tried not to bow under the weight of rejection.

And then Hurricane Katrina roared through my hometown, flattening the world, uprooting trees and asphalt roads, stringing houses across railroad tracks like pearls on a necklace. The storm surge bulldozed the coast and ripped people from rooftops and trees out to sea. The great storm drowned all. The wind howled.

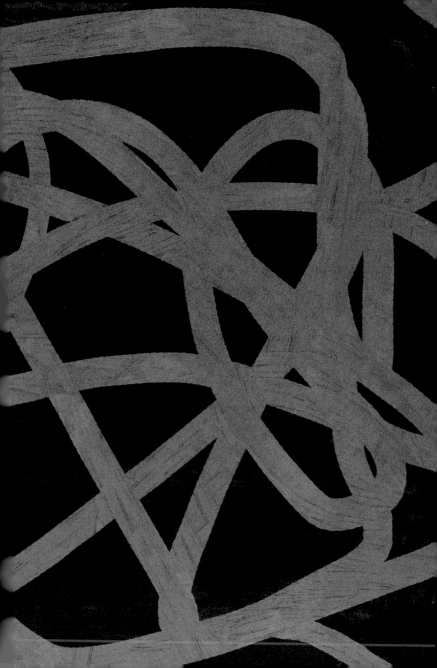

My family and I swam, scrambled, cowered, found shelter, and survived. Many who lived through the hurricane fled its aftermath, but instead of fleeing, I moved home to hard lessons. That relentless storm taught me that a natural disaster could occur at any time and not only erase the landscape that I loved but eviscerate my community as well. Learning that silenced me. Bewildered by hopelessness and helplessness, I almost gave up on writing. Why should I rebuild? Why should I insist on telling our stories?

But a little voice spoke inside of me: a stubborn, foolish, reckless, wise voice. *Don't give up*, it said. *Try one more time*, it said. And (because I was broken and desperate and yearned for hope) I listened.

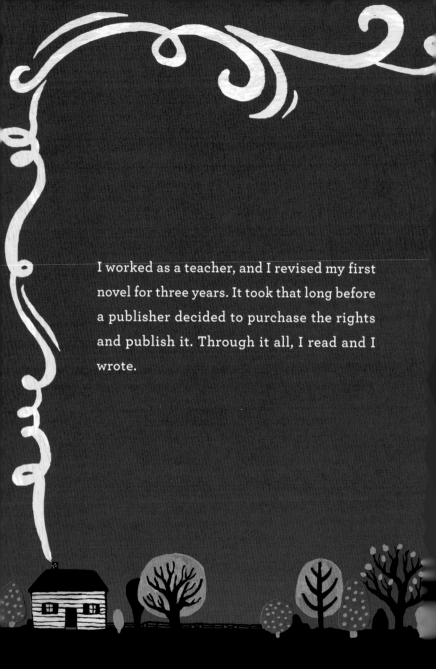

I worked as a teacher, and I revised my first novel for three years. It took that long before a publisher decided to purchase the rights and publish it. Through it all, I read and I wrote.

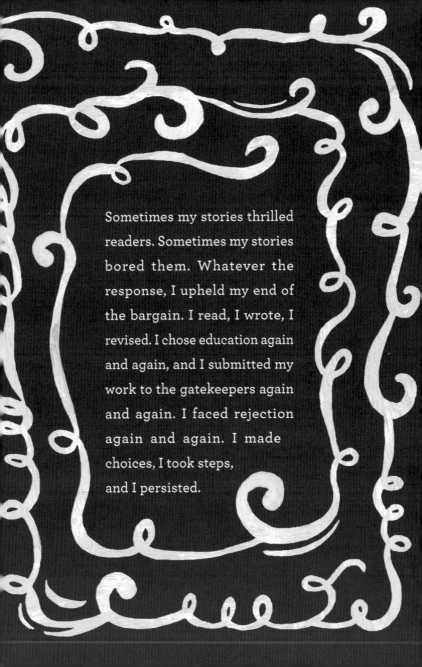

Sometimes my stories thrilled readers. Sometimes my stories bored them. Whatever the response, I upheld my end of the bargain. I read, I wrote, I revised. I chose education again and again, and I submitted my work to the gatekeepers again and again. I faced rejection again and again. I made choices, I took steps, and I persisted.

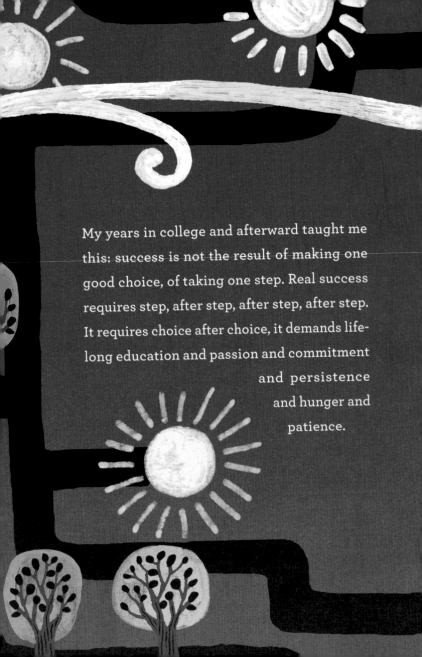

My years in college and afterward taught me this: success is not the result of making one good choice, of taking one step. Real success requires step, after step, after step, after step. It requires choice after choice, it demands life-long education and passion and commitment and persistence and hunger and patience.

And not the hunger that is easily sated, like the hunger for sweets that plagued me so when I was young, when I wanted instant success, when I wanted a lifetime of reward after four years of effort. Sometimes this kind of success happens for people: people like Zadie Smith and Edwidge Danticat, who are incredibly gifted writers, who bang out bestsellers in their early twenties.

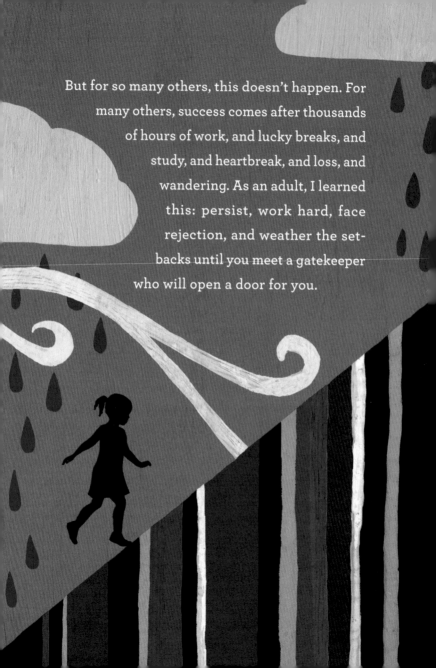

But for so many others, this doesn't happen. For many others, success comes after thousands of hours of work, and lucky breaks, and study, and heartbreak, and loss, and wandering. As an adult, I learned this: persist, work hard, face rejection, and weather the setbacks until you meet a gatekeeper who will open a door for you.

Sometimes, you are twenty when you stumble upon an open doorway. Sometimes, you are thirty. Sometimes you are forty, or fifty, or sixty. I remembered this when I felt like giving up, when I thought I'd pack all my notebooks and stories into plastic bags and put them away, when I thought I would resign them to the recycling bin.

And I remembered this new lesson I'd learned about persistence and success when I looked again at my parents, my uncles and aunts, all the people in my small, rural, black community who persisted, even with the promise of less on the horizon.

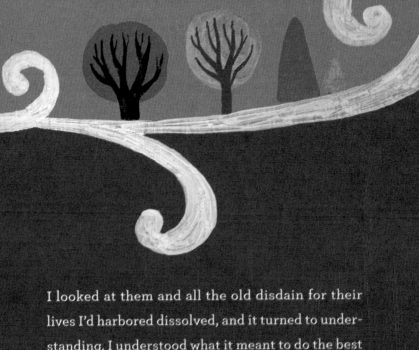

I looked at them and all the old disdain for their lives I'd harbored dissolved, and it turned to understanding. I understood what it meant to do the best you can with what you've been given.

For my grandmother, who only had a sixth-grade education, this meant educating herself in skills and trades as an adult. She studied to be a seamstress, a nurse's aide, a hairdresser, so she could support herself and her children. Success for her came when she was nearly fifty, when she gained employment in a pharmaceutical packing plant with health insurance, a competitive salary, enough money so that she didn't have to struggle to figure out how she would pay her bills, clothe and feed her children.

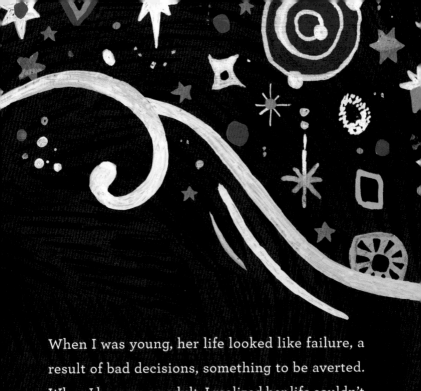

When I was young, her life looked like failure, a result of bad decisions, something to be averted. When I became an adult, I realized her life couldn't be described in such glib terms, that life was a tumultuous sea, and that my grandmother had spent her days afloat on a raft, and that she'd paddled and bailed water, and read the map of constellations in the sky to find land, reprieve, and to survive.

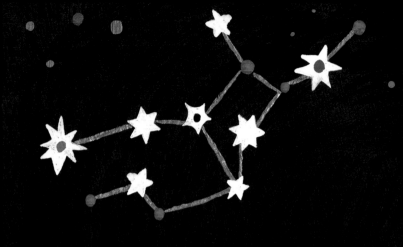

Be patient with yourself. If you are one of those lucky people who are exceptionally good at an endeavor they're passionate about, if you possess tireless ambition and keen direction right now, congratulations. You will go far and do well. Your successes will come early, and rapidly.

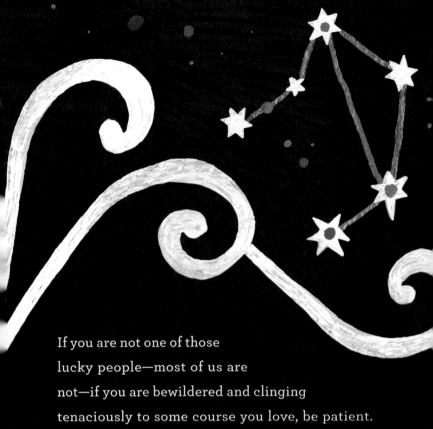

If you are not one of those
lucky people—most of us are
not—if you are bewildered and clinging
tenaciously to some course you love, be patient.
Work hard. Hold your dream tightly to you, and do
everything you can to realize it within reason. Take
a step that will lead you toward the realization of
your dream, and then take another, and another,
and another.

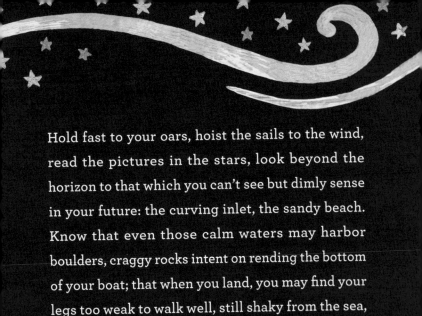

Hold fast to your oars, hoist the sails to the wind, read the pictures in the stars, look beyond the horizon to that which you can't see but dimly sense in your future: the curving inlet, the sandy beach. Know that even those calm waters may harbor boulders, craggy rocks intent on rending the bottom of your boat; that when you land, you may find your legs too weak to walk well, still shaky from the sea, and that the soil may have its own perils. But know that this is life.

And also know that the fruit on the trees is sweet, and warm to the mouth, as is life as well. Persist. Be patient. Be well.

Jesmyn Ward received her MFA from the University of Michigan and is currently a professor of creative writing at Tulane University. She is the author of the novels *Where the Line Bleeds*; *Salvage the Bones*, which won the 2011 National Book Award and was a finalist for the New York Public Library Young Lions Fiction Award and the Dayton Literary Peace Prize; and *Sing, Unburied, Sing*, which won the 2017 National Book Award and was a finalist for the Kirkus Prize, the PEN/Faulkner Award, the Los Angeles Times Book Prize, and the Andrew Carnegie Medal. She is also the editor of the anthology *The Fire This Time: A New Generation Speaks about Race* and the author of the memoir *Men We Reaped*, which was a finalist for the National Book Critics Circle Award and the Hurston/Wright Legacy Award and won the Chicago Tribune Heartland Prize and the Media for a Just Society Award. In 2017, she was awarded a MacArthur "genius grant." She lives in Mississippi with her family.

ABOUT THE ILLUSTRATOR

Gina Triplett is a widely acclaimed artist and illustrator. She creates imagery for a variety of outlets, including books, magazines, clothing, patterns, posters, murals, and other products. She works in pen, ink, and paint, and enjoys using them to create dynamic compositions of vivid color. When she's not working for clients she can be found drawing in her sketchbook or painting for gallery exhibitions. She lives and works in Philadelphia.